GHOST
STORIES
of
UPTOWN
GREENWOOD

To: Wyff + Janett
Thanks Gabrielle Barrett

GHOST STORIES

of

UPTOWN GREENWOOD

The History & Mystery of the South Carolina Lakelands

MARJORIE LANELLE

Palmetto Publishing Group, LLC
Charleston, SC

For information regarding special discounts for bulk purchases, please contact
Palmetto Publishing Group at Info@PalmettoPublishingGroup.com.

ISBN-13: 978-1-944313-93-7
ISBN-10: 1-944313-93-1

TABLE OF CONTENTS

INTRODUCTION

Nestled among the foothills of South Carolina, Greenwood County is located in the heart of the Piedmont region and is now referred to as part of the appropriately named area "the Lakelands."

Greenwood is proud to be the birthplace of several famous trailblazers and leaders such as educator Dr. Benjamin Mays, rhythm, blues, and beach band the Swingin' Medallions, Jazz saxophonist Odean Pope, and baseball legends Roselle Williams and Bill Voiselle.

Lander University and Piedmont Technical College call Greenwood home, and the Greenwood Genetic Center have made leaps and bounds into the future of modern medicine.

Award-winning festivals such as the South Carolina Festival of Flowers, the SC Festival of Stars (an Independence Day celebration), the Catfish Feastival, and the SC Festival of Discovery (BBQ and blues) have also been popular calling cards for this county.

As with all historical towns, Greenwood has several must-see landmarks. Among these are Cokesbury College, the Museum & Railroad Historical Center, the Civilian Conservation Corps Museum at the Drummond Center, the Ninety Six Historic Site (a Revolutionary War battlefield, aka Star Fort), and the historical Ninety Six Train Depot.

Lake Greenwood is a beautiful exhibit of nature and referred to as part of what is better known as the Freshwater Coast. This stunning lake borders not only one but three South Carolina counties: Newberry, Laurens, and Greenwood.

Founded in 1897, Greenwood has since been known for its lush vegetation and green appearance. For years and to some still today, Greenwood bannered the nickname "the Emerald City."

In recent history, the old "Downtown Greenwood" has gone through a major and beautiful transformation and is now known as "Uptown Greenwood." Renovations include but are not limited to establishing a historic district, new façades and streetscapes, a new farmers market, a splash pad, and several new restaurants and businesses.

The Emerald Triangle Project revamped the uptown area for the art district, which includes the Museum & Historical Railroad Center, the Greenwood Community Theatre, and the Arts Center of Greenwood. Venue options were also granted for live indoor and outdoor entertainment.

Year-round outdoor gardens and water features ring true to the new and exciting branded statement that "There's Always Something Blooming in Greenwood."

Although many of the changes and ideas are contemporary in design, the City of Greenwood's beautifully aged architectural buildings add magnificent and regal character to the town.

Continuous betterment and community involvement are top priorities for current city manager Charlie Barrineau and Mayor Welborn Adams, who work hand in hand with the Greenwood city and county councils, the Greenwood Chamber of Commerce, uptown merchants, and citizens to ensure

Uptown Greenwood is not only maintained but that future plans of prosperity are kept in motion.

Tourists and locals alike are continuously drawn to this small yet busy hub. Even though Uptown Greenwood is now a perfect blend and balance of modern, upscale dining and shopping, it still retains its small-town feel and is saturated with true Southern hospitality.

All this being said, one must remember that even when small-town Americana ages and changes, there is one thing that seems to remain the same: each and every town comes with its own unique folklore, ghost stories, strange happenings, and even unexplained phenomena; mysterious magnets that seem to attract even the biggest skeptics. There are always stories of things that go bump in the night, goings-on with no logical explanation, and maybe even silly little incidents that can make one question one's sanity, and Uptown Greenwood is no exception! Yes, it has its own intriguing stories and this book is part of a series that will include the history and mystery of the SC Lakelands.

In Uptown Greenwood, one may be tapped upon the shoulder by an unseen visitor or could even encounter a stern, transparent gentleman dressed in period clothing. One may feel a cold breeze sweep by even on the hottest, most humid Southern summer day. Quiet whispers that tickle one's ear have also been experienced, caused by what seems to be invisible entities. As you can see, when it comes to the history and mystery of the Lakelands of South Carolina, Uptown Greenwood will surely not disappoint!

If you decide to mosey on over to Uptown Greenwood for a visit, remember to bring a camera and a friend, as you won't want to experience this alone.

"Some say that they have to *see* in order to believe, while others feel that one must *believe* in order to see," said author Marjorie LaNelle. Either way, you are now invited to sit back, relax, and enjoy your visit to this lovely Southern town as you read and meet the ghosts of Uptown Greenwood.

CHAPTER ONE

FLOWERS FOR SALE

It was a crisp yet sunny autumn day. There was a slight breeze that made the fallen leaves dance a rustled jig, but there were still more leaves on the trees than on the ground, as it was still early fall. What I vividly remember about the weather that day was that the sunshine seemed to make the golden leaves remaining on the trees in the uptown area almost glow. The sun was, indeed, bright.

It was lovely in Greenwood this time of year. I seldom drove through town on my way home from work because I lived about eleven miles away and using the by-pass was a quicker way to my house, but for that day, it was a nice and welcomed change of scenery.

The traffic light turned yellow, so I began to slow down. There were no cars beside me in the right lane or behind me, so I just took a deep breath and continued to slowly roll to a complete stop. As I sat there, I kept enjoying nature's ambiance right there in the middle of town. That was one of the enjoyments of living in a small Southern town. This was my time to relax and decide what I would cook for supper when I got home.

I rolled my front two windows down to breathe in a little bit of fresh air. You see, I'd been raised in the country for several years of my life, and I loved fresh air. It reminded me of home, when I was a child.

As I sat there, I looked to my left and waved at a passerby (because that was what we did in South Carolina—we waved at just about everybody; it was what we Southerners referred to as "Southern hospitality"). The gentleman waved back, stuck a folded newspaper under his arm, and picked up his pace to cross the street in front of my car.

I looked to the right and saw a young woman walking back and forth in front of one of the local shops. She was carrying a curved basket of freshly cut spring flowers, and she wore a long, colonial-style cotton dress. It was white with what seemed to be tiny blue flowers spaced perfectly every few inches. I assumed she was selling her flowers and that her dress was part of a smart marketing strategy. It had sure gotten my attention! She had long, brown hair that was loosely pulled back with a blue bow in the center of the back of her head.

What struck me as odd was that her flowers were daffodils, tulips, and daises—*spring* flowers, and here we were in fall. I looked on around farther to the right and noticed that the corner store was a florist, so now it all made sense.

The young lady paced back and forth in front of the shop beside the florist. I looked up to read the name of the shop: the Two Old Bags. I giggled to myself as I said the name out loud and shook my head. What a silly but great name, and yet another wonderful marketing strategy.

As I looked back over to the flower girl, she stopped and turned from the waist to look straight at me. She then, with a smile, motioned with her hand as if to say, "Come here please and buy a flower." She picked up a daffodil (my favorite flower) and stretched out her arm as if to hand it to me.

BEEEEEP! The car that had driven up behind me loudly blew its horn. I hadn't realized that the light had turned green, and I thought I might have even peed a little. I was startled and a mighty bit ticked off. So off I drove, slowly—very slowly—just because the man behind me had been so rude as to lay on his horn. That was something we didn't do here in the South. He quickly passed me, showing me that I was number one (with his middle finger).

But, being the refined, Southern woman I was, I wasn't going to let him ruin my beautiful day. So I simply said, "Bless your heart," with a friendly and apologetic wave and whispered a little prayer under my breath for him. Yes, it was sincere . . . as sincere as I could be at the moment.

I drove for about half a block and turned my right blinker on to switch lanes. I had made up my mind that I was going back to buy some flowers. I just had to—at least one daffodil! After all, that young woman had been dedicated to her mission, and I was sure that as soon as she sold her flowers, she could go home to her family. Heck! I thought I might even buy the whole basket of flowers! But then again, that would depend on how much they were, because payday was still three days away.

As I made my way back to the storefront of the Two Old Bags, I saw that the only parking space was in front of the bookstore a few doors down. I no longer saw the flower girl. I walked down to the corner of the street and headed toward the florist, but it was already closed for the day. This very strange feeling came over me. I didn't understand; I had just seen her less than a minute ago! *Where is she?* I asked myself.

I put my thinking cap on and began to have a silent conversation with myself. Maybe she worked for the Two Old Bags; after all, that was the store she'd been pacing back and forth in front of. Yes, I'd try there. So in I went. As I opened the heavy glass door to enter, a bell rang. The bell's sound reminded me of going to the general store with my mama when I'd been a child. I hadn't heard that sound in years. It felt good.

I pretended to be a customer. I looked around and realized I was surrounded by a sea of beads. Yes, beads: thousands upon thousands of neatly organized beads. Every size and every color you could think of. There were beads in glass bowls, beads in wine glasses, and beads in candleholders, all clear containers, filled with beads. I was sure that the Two Old Bags was a shop where you could come and learn to make your own jewelry and other crafts.

I was greeted by a friendly voice from a table in the back: "Hello! What can I help you find?"

I didn't see anyone and thought maybe it was the flower girl. Then I saw the woman who matched the voice, and she was definitely not the flower girl. She introduced herself as Sandy Smith, co-owner of the Two Old Bags. She explained that she and her twin sister, Susan, owned the craft and beading shop. Sandy was about five feet two inches tall, maybe five feet three, and jolly in stature as well as in personality. I instantly liked her. She began to tell me about classes that were held there to learn how to "bead" and make one's own jewelry.

During her pitch, her twin sister arrived. Yep, they were identical all right! We became instant friends, as our souls just seemed to click.

I smelled the scent of hay and melted iron. I assumed that with crafts they may have been using a soldering iron, but the smell of hay...well, I couldn't explain that. But then something else caught my attention. I noticed a tall, thin man, sharply dressed in a brown three-piece suit. He was also wearing black, shiny dress shoes and a brown hat. He peeked out from behind a curtain and took a step to the left so he was right in the middle of the doorway. He just stood there, not uttering a word. I assumed he was an employee, their much-older brother or their father, but I didn't ask.

That strange feeling came over me again, and simultaneously I heard an almost deafening high-pitched noise in my left ear. As I walked toward the back of the store to get a closer look at the man, I pretended to shop. With each step I took, the man seemed to get more and more transparent. I could see the detailed pinstripes on his brown suit, but I could only make out limited details of his face. I walked closer to see him, and he just vanished! I felt a swoosh of wind pass by me and heard what sounded like bird's wings flying. At this point, I thought I'd gone crazy. Yep, I was pretty sure of it. I was also sure that I looked startled, because I was.

I composed myself and asked for the price of a gourd that had a sunflower painted on it. I was sure one of the owners answered me, but I couldn't focus enough to listen.

I finally got up the nerve to ask Sandy and Susan about the flower girl who had been selling flowers in front of their building. I asked if she worked for them or the florist next door. The puzzled look on their faces and strange smiles they gave each other answered my question. I was sure that they, too, thought I had really lost my mind. All I could imagine was hearing the "cuckoo" sound made by a cuckoo clock. I was sure they both thought I was some kind of drunken lunatic who had wandered in off the streets. So before they could decide to call the police or, worse, the mental hospital, I said, "Thank you," and headed for the front door.

"Please don't leave," begged Susan as she grabbed my arm. "Come, sit down and tell us what all you saw."

This was when they shared with me that there were other

strange goings-on in their building. As we three talked for what seemed like hours, I once again saw the gentleman in the brown suit walk across the back of the store. Oblivious to us, he went through the back doorway, never to reappear while I was there. I described what I had seen, and they simultaneously said, "Oh, we call him Mr. Friendly," and looked at each other and chuckled.

"Ummm . . . Mr. Friendly?" I asked. "Please, please do explain."

"Well, yeah, we call him Mr. Friendly!" answered Sandy.

Susan elbowed her sister as if to tell her to shut up, as they might have already shared too much with this friendly stranger; after all, they didn't usually discuss their strange experiences with anyone other than each other. Anytime they did, they ran the risk of people thinking they were both crazy. The duo had chalked it up to being a "twin thing." But now they knew that others could also sense what they were experiencing.

"Well, we've never seen him," explained Susan, "but we can feel him sometimes."

Sandy piped in, "Things seem to go missing, too, and we often hear what sounds like dropped objects, yet we can never find anything that has fallen!"

The intriguing conversation continued. I not only learned of their strange occurrences but about them as well, and I really liked these two ladies. Needless to say, from then on, I became a regular customer, and we became lifelong friends.

Over the next several years, the paranormal activity seemed to increase and grow more and more frequent. Other customers, passers-by, and even relatives shared stories of odd happenings in this shop. One interesting story was that of seeing people sitting along the basement wall of the building. It was discovered through research of the owners that this particular building had once served as a fallout shelter during the 1940s and 1950s, which could possibly explain this experience!

During this time, the top floor, which had been used for storage, was renovated and converted into an apartment. More strange and unusual things began to happen there as well. The only access to the apartment was the stairs on the side of the building, on which heavy footsteps were often heard even when no one could be seen. A dark shadow had reportedly been seen (from Main Street below-looking up), walking back and forth in front of the top floor's windows. Visitors to the apartment often had the feeling of someone or something watching them, which could be "quite disturbing and spooky," as described by one paranormal investigator who had obtained audio evidence of the phantom footsteps on the stairs and across the floor in the apartment.

Several paranormal investigation teams were allowed to conduct inspections. Among the evidence collected and presented to the twins were ghostly photos and recordings of disembodied voices. There were over a dozen strangers who were drawn to the location by unseen forces and who supplied unsolicited ghostly information to the twins. Stories of a little ghost girl, a dog who had passed on, and many other sightings and encounters with Mr. Friendly, and even a parrot!

The sisters had never felt afraid or threatened by the spirits that seemed to inhabit their shop, and they welcomed anyone to the Two Old Bags who wanted to stop in, visit, shop, or just say hello.

Being intrigued not by the stories but because of my personal experiences, I decided to conduct a little research of my own, and here is what I learned: in 1898, the area that is now known as 204 Main Street served as a parking spot for buggies that were being repaired by the local buggy shop. Located one store over from the corner of Main Street and Oregon Avenue, this area was nothing but dirt at the time, and after the invention and gradual influx of automobiles, it was converted into an automotive repair and garage, still with a dirt floor.

In 1914, twin structures were built on the dirt foundation, and over the years, several businesses had been housed in this particular building. A grocery store, a general mercantile store, a shoe store, a boutique, and an organics shop were among both the successful and short-lived businesses.

For years, the twin buildings shared a doorway that connected them, but within the past few decades, that doorway had been covered over. Though the two buildings were still a twin structure, from that point on they would be two individual structures housing separate businesses.

Today, coincidentally, twin entrepreneurs Susan and Sandy Smith, along with a former business partner; currently own one side of the twin buildings. This part of the twin structure has more than its share of ghostly sightings!

CHAPTER TWO

THE GHOSTS OF GCT

On a cool September evening during the 1980s, a young amateur actress was scheduled to meet with the seamstress of Greenwood Community Theatre on the top floor of the building. She was to be fitted for the costume she would wear in an upcoming play. The seamstress informed the actress that she had to make a quick phone call and would meet her upstairs in a few minutes. The actress continued to climb the stairs leading to the costume room, admiring the sparkling, glitter-filled ceiling along the way.

Like any young teenage girl would, she held costume after costume up to her body and pretended to be many people as she waited. As she hummed and danced with an old, beautiful, blue-sequined party dress, she heard the faint sound of a baby crying. She looked around, reasoning that the noise was probably coming from outside, as the theater was located directly on Main Street and the window and walls were the only things separating the theater from the sidewalk. She dismissed the crying and continued to dance with the dress, curtsying to her mannequin partner, who stood there silently. As she placed a tiara on her head and pulled long white gloves up above her elbows, she admired herself in the large mirror that was propped up against the wall.

Once again, she picked up the evening gown which transformed her into royalty. She noticed that other than the crinkling of the crinoline netting that was sewn into the evening gown, the room was silent. But then she heard the baby crying again. *Maybe it's just a cat in the alley,* she thought. But as the crying continued, she became convinced that it *was* the sound of a baby. Growing more and more concerned by the minute, the young actress called out for the seamstress; no one answered. *Maybe someone came into the lobby downstairs, and they have a baby with them,* she thought and ignored the cries for as long as she possibly could. They seemed to be closer now and grew louder by the minute.

With chills now running up and down her spine, she suddenly realized she might not actually be alone! The crying continued. A feeling of dread came over her; she now felt shaken and a bit afraid, and looking to either side of her, she began to nervously sing her favorite upbeat show tune.

This steadied her, and she laid the dress on top of a chest and turned to listen more closely so she could find out just *where* the cries were coming from. As she began to follow the sound, the cries seemed to grow louder and louder, yet still sounded as if they were coming from inside a tunnel; the louder the cries became, the more of an echo they created. Her nervous singing was now down to a very faint hum, and she focused all her attention on the cries.

As she slid some dusty men's suits across their rack, she revealed a somewhat dark corner in the room. It was hard at first for her to see, but then what she saw became very clear. Sitting in the corner was what appeared to be a young, transparent girl dressed in 1950s-style clothing, wearing Oxford shoes, and thick, white, turned-down bobby socks. The girl was scrunched up, almost in the fetal position on the old wooden floor. She appeared to be very afraid, with tears streaming down her petrified face as she swaddled a screaming baby in what looked to be a letterman sweater. The new mother was uncontrollably shaking, not knowing what to do with the newborn to which she had obviously just given birth.

Stunned, the young actress stood motionless and confused, not knowing what exactly was going on. Logically, this couldn't be explained. She questioned her sanity and then tried to scream, but nothing came out. She could not move. She could not breathe. She could do nothing but stare and try to justify what her eyes were seeing, which was impossible!

Just then, she heard the seamstress walking up the stairs, announcing in a peppy voice, "Well, let's get you fitted!"

The actress turned to glance at the seamstress and then quickly looked back to the corner. The ghostly duo was gone, and the crying had ceased. The young actress began to cry and tried to explain her story to the seamstress, who simply laughed and marked it up to the young girl's imagination.

This incident has never been explained, but to this day, people still report hearing the cries of a baby. Did a young girl really give birth in that costume on the top floor in the 1950s, or was it just the vivid imagination of a very creative, young actress?

The Phantom Cigarette Smoke

In early 2009 an older prominent lady and gentleman (who wish to remain anonymous) entered into the lobby of the Greenwood Community Theatre to pick up their reserved tickets for the evening from the ticket window; they were the first ones to arrive that night. They handed the usher their tickets, and the three headed into the theater through the door on the right side of the lobby.

As the lady entered the auditorium, she angrily stated, "I can't believe that after all of the money that was spent on making this theater this beautiful, someone would be allowed to smoke in here!"

Confused, the usher asked what she meant, explaining that it was a smoke-free facility. Just then he, too, caught the strong aroma of cigarette smoke and quickly assured and reassured her that he would find the culprit and put a stop to the situation. But after searching for several minutes, he could find no one smoking in or around the theater, and after a few moments, the smell was gone.

On several occasions since then, there have been recurring incidents of phantom cigarette smoke that can be distinctly smelled, most strongly near the right-hand lobby door.

Oddly enough, actors and actresses have also reported that while rehearsing or during a performance, as they looked to the back left of the theater (which is located at the entrance of the right lobby door), they saw the tall, dark figure of a gentleman standing among the seats, as if the seats weren't even there, and he appeared to be smoking a cigarette. This translucent male figure has been spotted both when the theater is empty as well as when the seats are filled.

Current GCT box office manager Angela Scott recalled her own experience: "My encounter with the smell of tobacco was while I was standing at the right entrance to the auditorium. This would be my first of many unexplainable experiences." She has worked at the theater for several years and spent countless hours there, and she went on to say that her most memorable encounter was of smelling "the sweetest and strongest hint of tobacco I have ever smelled" when she was the only one in the building. "And still, to this day," she added, "children from the theater workshops will come to me from time to time and say, 'Ms. Angela, you may want to check; I think someone is smoking in the here!'" Angela has never been able to identify the culprit or explain the odd yet very distinct aroma.

Other haunted happenings at the historic theater have taken place on the stage as well as in the basement, which now serves as a dressing and green room during live productions. Here, as well as on stage during performances, props have mysteriously disappeared and then reappeared in places they should never have been. There have been reports of lights dimming on and off on their own, disembodied voices on the lower level, and mysterious whispers that seem to come from the orchestra pit. Some witnesses have even reported feeling someone unseen caressing, stroking, or gently pulling their hair before going on stage. Others have heard footsteps on the side stairs as well as on the catwalk when the theater was otherwise empty.

Could the history of the building explain any of these strange happenings? You will have to determine that for yourself as you either visit the theater or continue to read on.

Live performances in Greenwood officially began in the year 1930 with what was then known as the Little Theater. Under the auspices of the American Legion Auxiliary, the theater's rendition of *The Brat*, held in the Greenwood High School Auditorium, was the first production and the beginning of what is now known as GCT.[1]

Originally known as the State Theatre, the GCT building itself was built in 1934, and the theater was founded in 1954, at that time named the Greenwood Little Theatre. At one time, it was even known as the Jerry Lewis Theater. Rumor had it that

1 Donald McKellar, *GCT and Me (Greenwood, SC: The Attic Press, Inc., 1999), 6.*

a young, single, teenage girl gave birth to a baby on the top floor of a nearby building (possibly the current GCT building); and although that story has never been substantiated, it could still be true. Being single and pregnant in the 1950s been considered shameful and embarrassing to family members and was not spoken of.

Later, the three-story building fell into disrepair, so the theater was housed on Kirksey Drive. In 2007, the theater was renovated with state-of-the-art equipment as part of the $1.2 million Emerald Triangle Project. It is now located at its original location of 110 Main Street as part of the Emerald Triangle Cultural Arts District of Uptown Greenwood.

Over the years, thousands upon thousands of people have entered the doors of the structure to be entertained by live plays, movies on the silver screen, meetings, musical productions, concerts, and even political events.

Could the smoking man be a patron who enjoys watching live theater, even in the afterlife? Or could he be a former director or actor who so loved the theater that he has made it his eternal residence? This is as far as speculation has taken me, but it remains clear that the GCT building has its share of supernatural occurrences!

CHAPTER THREE

UNSEEN GUESTS

Serving as the gateway into the City of Greenwood, the Inn on the Square is currently the only hotel located in the uptown area. The large, pale-green building houses over forty rooms, a bar, a ballroom, a conference room, a laundry area, and a restaurant.

It is located on the corner of Main Street and East Court Avenue, and this particular area of land has been home to over a dozen businesses. A tire shop, a furniture store, and a funeral home are among prior establishments. This building has not always been just one building. Years ago, there were two buildings with an alleyway separating them, and where the asphalt road now lies beside and in front of the hotel was once just dirt and part of what had been deemed the world's widest main street. Railroad tracks ran parallel to the building as well.

Over the years, the inn has had its share of ghostly happenings, and following are the ones that have most recently been experienced.

The "Walk-In"

A video surveillance camera captured a gentleman patron walking up to the check-in desk to speak with a clerk. As the guest stood there, what is referred to as a *walk-in* ghost was seen walking into the frame of the recording. The unknown and transparent figure seemed to literally step into the man's body and take his shape. After conducting his business, the man walked away from the counter, but the unknown figure remained in the shape of the man who had just walked away. Within the next few seconds, the figure dissipated and simply vanished. The video still exists and is in the care of a former employee who now lives in a neighboring state.

Neither the clerk nor the man has any recollection of the experience. It was as if they were oblivious to the entire event.

Bill, the Resident Ghost

Bill is the most well-known ghost at the inn. Newspaper articles and newscasts have featured this mischievous entity. He has been spotted more than any other.

On many occasions, usually in the evening hours, a handsome, transparent gentleman wearing a gray, pinstriped, three-piece suit was spotted standing in the corner of the Fox & Hound Lounge, which is the bar inside the inn. This particular ghostly gentleman has been seen on numerous occasions by many folks (those drinking *and* those who had consumed no alcohol at all). This spirit is simply referred to as "Bill," and employees and patrons alike have experienced this apparition over many decades, usually in the same area of the inn.

Former owners invited a local intuitive to visit the hotel.

Without being given any information, she sensed the spirit of a man there by the name of William. "But his friends call him Bill," she said with a smile. "He was a successful businessman, and he loved to smoke cigars."

According to the woman, Bill had fallen ill and had been waiting on a train that would have taken him to his family, but being too weak to run to catch it, he had missed the boarding time by mere seconds and had to wait for the next train, which wouldn't be running for hours. Bill's condition had continued to deteriorate, and sadly, he died before the next train was scheduled to arrive.

Bill now not only resides in the inn but is something of a prankster, tapping patrons on the shoulder, making the television in the bar fall off the wall from where it was mounted, and banging on the bar doors after they were locked for the night. He has also been known to slightly move glasses filled with alcohol across the bar at times, with scotch seeming to be his favorite. Bill, although mischievous, is deemed to be harmless. The faint smell of cigars is noticeable from time to time, even when the bar is empty. Keys and other small items have been taken and then returned moments later to their last-known spot. Up until this point, Bill has only been seen, not heard.

In the distant past, Greenwood was known as a busy railroad hub, and its depot was located directly beside where the Inn on the Square now sits. The rails that once ran through town have long been taken up, and the depot has long been gone. There are, however, trains that run adjacent to the uptown area, just a few blocks from the inn. Several past employees noticed that Bill sometimes appeared more frequently when the roar of the rails could be heard or felt, and he was especially active when the train whistle bellowed, maybe in hopes of catching that next train to take him home.

The Restaurant

The restaurant area of the inn holds a much darker story. The inn has been closed several times over the last few decades and has been used for other purposes. It was once a place of housing for students who attended the local university. It is believed that during this period, some rituals were performed that invited unwelcome spiritual guests into the hotel.

The owner at the time asked a local paranormal team to come in and investigate. There was no electricity in the building, as the establishment had been closed for over a year, yet a radio started to play in the restaurant area during the team's visit. The radio had no batteries in it, and it was not plugged in.

Also, at least three investigators saw what they described as a black yet transparent creature with the body of a man but the facial features and head of a horse. Chortles, neighs, and even a growl were actually caught on a recorder during this particular examination. It seemed that the creature was contained in a side room and did not wander the building; it was almost as if it were in an invisible cage. The investigators agreed that this creature was of an evil nature. It seemed to just be walking back and forth on all fours in the contained area, never acknowledging its current surroundings in present time. The building was smudged with sage, and the investigation team bestowed Native American and Christian blessings upon the building.

No guests have reported encountering this being, nor has it been seen or heard since.

The Three

The third floor of the inn has its own unexplained sightings of lost spirits. Several guests as well as one employee who quickly quit and never returned have said they saw a little girl, a young woman, and an elderly lady roaming the halls.

During the same paranormal investigation mentioned in the previous section, a ball was placed in the hall on the third floor. After a short while, the ball reportedly began to move, as if being rolled down the hallway by a child.

Each time this ghostly trio is seen, its members are all present together. On one occasion, a guest woke up around 3:00 a.m., and there, at the foot of the bed, were all three female entities. They made no sound; they reportedly just stood there, staring at the guest. Within seconds, they disappeared.

Other guests and employees have allegedly heard a little girl's voice singing the song "Rain, Rain, Go Away" as well as faint giggles.

The Storage Room

To the back right of the bottom floor is a storage room that was once utilized as a laundry room, among other things. A patron and Greenwood resident by the name of Jimmy Mack conducted a walk-through of the building during its most recent renovation. As he walked through the storage room, he smelled a curiously distinct and pungent aroma. It seemed he was the only one who smelled it. He described it as similar to the scent of formaldehyde, which is used widely as embalming fluid for the deceased. Jimmy Mack discussed this with one of the employees. As it turns out, the storage room had once been a morgue!

"I have experienced many things in this place," explained Mack. "I have seen shadows move across the bar, sensed a dark, repressed entity in the restaurant, and witnessed the video of a female spirit walking into the bar, seemingly looking around for someone and then turning back around to leave. The strange thing about this video was it was in the early 2000s, and she was dressed in clothes from the 1950s. There was also only a torso . . . she had no body from the waist down. Now that was most bizarre!"

Going Up?

A traveling couple explained that after stepping into the hotel elevator and pressing the button for the second floor, they were taken to the third floor instead. As the doors opened and they started to step out, they realized they weren't where they were supposed to be. The elevator doors had already closed, and the couple reported hearing whispers of conversation but couldn't make out the words. They tried to get back on the elevator, but after waiting for about ten minutes, they decided it must be broken and took the stairs instead.

After they arrived at their proper room on the second floor, their aggravation continued to mount as after several attempts, the key to the door would not work. Frustrated, the couple left their luggage in the hallway, and as the man went to notify the clerk, the lady returned to their car to retrieve her coat.

The clerk and the man returned to the room to see that the door was no longer locked and a small piece of luggage was propping the door open. When the lady returned with her coat just a few minutes later, they were all puzzled as to what had happened. To this day, that incident cannot be explained.

The Lobby

The lobby of this lovely hotel is where an alley once divided the two buildings before they were merged into one. It is large, welcoming, and majestically decorated. Above the center of the lobby and directly in front of the check-in area is an opening that's surrounded by the second- and third-floor balconies. Several colorful flags adorn the balconies.

Unexplained breezes can be felt when there are no doors or windows open. A previously employed night auditor who wishes to remain anonymous described the breezes to be "slight, cold, and just enough to make the flags sway a little . . . but enough to make a person shiver."

A local ordained minister, Reverend Ann Dowis used to work at the Inn on the Square. Here is what she had to say about the reputedly haunted hotel: "As a former employee of the Inn on the Square, I can honestly say, without a doubt, that paranormal activity does occur within these walls." Reverend Dowis is convinced by her own experiences that "this building is alive with death." She went on to explain that she had experienced everything from unexplained moving objects to temperature changes, disembodied voices, strange odors, and even feeling the touch of unseen entities. "There were many times I had the feeling of being watched. The spirits like to play games as well. For example, I would receive phone calls from empty offices, and there were too many occasions to count where invisible footsteps could be heard. The Inn on the Square in Uptown Greenwood is quite the amusement park for spirits."

CHAPTER FOUR

MAYHEM AT THE MUSEUM

Located at 106 Main Street, the Greenwood Museum has its own share of spooky and unique happenings. The museum has been housed in this building since 1982 and was most recently renovated as part of the Emerald Triangle Project in the early 2000s.

The structure has a top floor, which is rented out for events; a middle floor, which is level with the sidewalk and acts as the main floor/storefront; and a bottom level, which is the basement. The museum also has its own elevator to help visitors maneuver from floor to floor.

This building not only holds many collections of antique, historic, and interesting items but also seems to hold just as many stories of strange goings-on. Some people believe that items and physical matter can "house" residual energy and that a museum is just the place for that energy to manifest itself.

According to past and present employees and volunteers of the museum, the elevator seems to have a life of its own. It has been reported that the elevator doors will randomly open and close when there is no one in or around to manually press the control buttons. It's as if there is an invisible someone catering to the museum guests.

"While I was there," shared former employee Bethany Wade, "I had a weird feeling when I was in the collections room. I was working down there one day, and I could have sworn that I heard sighing or breathing; I felt nervous. Another odd thing was that the elevator would run up and down by itself when no one else was in the building, and the [elevator] doors would randomly open. We [employees] had several people tell us they, too, had experiences [in the museum]."

A former curator who wishes to remain anonymous insists that there were many occasions where patrons of the museum would walk up to the elevator to push the button, but before they could do so, the doors would open on their own, as if there were an unseen bellhop there to escort them to the next floor.

"There are even occasional mysterious phone calls that come through the elevator's sound system," stated current museum director Karen Jennings, who added and believes that this is "an effective way for disembodied beings to communicate!"

Museum volunteer and former director of tourism Jennifer Donlon saw a translucent male worker in the museum on a regular basis. "Well, he appeared in several areas, always wearing work clothes—like coveralls," Jennifer described. "He was about five foot nine or five foot ten and of average build." She continued by saying the transparent visitor would regularly appear to her in the afternoons between the months of March and June. "Even on Saturday mornings as well," she explained, "he would, at times, appear in the same room I was working in, but mainly he would just walk past the door to the archives room in the basement. Sometimes I would catch a glimpse of him by the cotton machine that was on display, or standing by the antique horse carriage. He never made a sound—always silent; I distinctly remember *that*. He pointed once to the steam pipe, and on another occasion he pointed to the front wall. I asked the curator of the museum at the time if anything was happening in that area of the museum." The curator informed Jennifer that the wall had been leaking and was soon going to be repaired by employees of the city. So that could explain why the apparition had pointed in the direction of the wall. "But I'm not sure just why he was pointing to the closed-off steam pipe. Maybe he was a steam pipe worker? That's still a mystery to me," concluded Jennifer.

The Soggy Footprints That Led to Nowhere

One of the most mysterious stories of the museum is that of the wet footprints. With the building being so old, it hasn't always been a museum. Several other businesses have occupied the space, and one can only imagine the variety of people who have hung around on the premises, especially since it is so close to the still-active railroad tracks that run adjacent to the building.

The bottom floor still has a bell system in place for deliveries. Years ago, when a delivery was being made to a business, the courier would press the bell on the outside of the delivery door. Though still intact, this system hasn't been used in over a decade. Most aren't even aware that the delivery bell system is still operational, but oh, is it ever!

One afternoon in the recent past, a museum employee heard the bell ring. Being that the museum no longer utilizes the bell system, she was surprised by the sound. Nonetheless, she hopped on the elevator to see who was at the basement door. To her surprise, when she opened the door there was no one there, so even though she was puzzled, she closed the door and locked it, figuring there were possibly some children from the local neighborhood just playing around.

As she turned to get back on the elevator and head up to the main floor, she noticed some wet footprints leading from the delivery door to the center of the room. Startled, she stood motionless, wondering where the unseen intruder might be hiding. At that point, she was sure she wasn't alone, but she knew no one had come in through the door when she opened it and in addition that it wasn't raining outside. She simply could not logically figure out what was happening. Looking back at the footprints, she noticed again how odd it was that they just stopped in the center of the room. They seemed to lead to, well . . . nowhere! With the hair on the back of her neck standing up and chills overcoming her body, she scurried back to the elevator, pushing the buttons frantically. Needless to say, she was spooked!

She shared the story with her fellow employees, and from then on they all began to think twice before going to the basement floor (or anywhere else in the museum) alone.

Silhouette of a Lady

The basement of the museum is now used as an educational science area. One of the most popular exhibits is a light machine that can "capture" one's shadow. People of all ages enjoy this machine.

On one occasion, the machine not only captured the shadow of a young boy but also the silhouette of a tall, thin lady. Reportedly, the young man could physically see the woman, but no one else in his family could. He told his mother that the lady was very tall, and he described her as wearing clothes like the ones women wore in cowboy movies. He also said she was carrying a large cloth bag and an umbrella.

Others have allegedly seen this woman walking in different areas of the building; all state that she was wearing period clothing.

Was she a traveler from the past, waiting on a train? Was she a spirit attached to an antique object now housed in the museum? Or could she just be a lost spirit, still wandering and trapped in a spiritual time capsule? No matter why she's here, this quiet lady doesn't seem to want to harm anyone.

CHAPTER FIVE

RUTH

Allura Bella Boutique (formerly Uptown Pizzazz) has become a very popular shopping destination for ladies of all ages, and because of its ghostly happenings, it has also become a well-sought-after paranormal hot spot!

Located at 308 Main Street in Uptown Greenwood, this building was constructed in the late 1800s and opened as a shoe shop. Throughout history, it has also been a men's clothing store, a camera shop, a bath and gift shop, and now, for the last several years, a ladies' boutique.

As hauntingly mysterious events began to happen, it was sensed that the ghost was female. Former owner of Uptown Pizzazz Jill Lawrence gave her the name 'Ruth'. Jill insisted there were unexplainable things that continued to happen in this location. Never feeling threatened or afraid, she explained that she was just a bit confused and taken aback at the ghostly goings-on.

"On one occasion, a designer handbag lifted off a shelf, moved out into midair, and was placed, upright, onto the floor below, never hitting or touching anything in its path," Jill explained. "This particular incident occurred after hours and was caught on the shop's security camera."

This same incident has reportedly happened again with the new owner! Yes, yet another floating purse was captured on a surveillance video camera after the shop had closed for the evening. These incidents have yet to be explained.

Another strange experience took place during the holiday season. A large, expensive nutcracker was securely on display on a round, wooden table at the front of the shop. Jill, the owner at the time, was in the back of the store when she heard a thud and then what sounded like a crash. As she hurried to the front of the boutique, she noticed that the heirloom nutcracker was now on the floor. Being that there were several items on the table with the nutcracker, the only explanation was that it had literally lifted up, floated through the air, and fallen to the floor. It had landed several feet away from the table, as if it were thrown or knocked off purposely. Just as with the purses, the nutcracker fell without disturbing anything in its direct path, "which was just not possible," said Jill as she shook her head. "The table was filled with other merchandise, and if the nutcracker had simply fallen over or been knocked over, it would have landed horizontally, hitting, breaking, and/or taking other items to the floor with it." She remains baffled to this day. "Ruth just must not have liked the nutcracker," she joked.

The Garden Room in the back of the shop also has its very own paranormal activity, seemingly unrelated to that of the front of the showroom. The beautiful, original wood flooring is still intact and seems to be home to ghostly footsteps, as there have been reports of squeaking floors when no one is there—at least no one who can be seen.

Jill has shared that she would periodically hear the voice of a lady calling her name, but when she answered, no one was there. On one occasion, she was working in the back of the store and heard a woman call her name from the front of the store; Jill yelled, "Coming!" But when she got to the main area of the floor, she could find no one.

CHAPTER SIX

CAPTURED ON FILM

Rudd's Camera and Video is located in the heart of Uptown Greenwood at 318 Main Street. Built in 1892, this particular building has in the past been the home of McClellan's Department Store and the Greenback Stamp Shop. It has housed Rudd's Camera and Video as well as the Frame Shop since 1979.

The building itself doesn't have any ghostly inhabitants that have been recorded, but it does have a unique and mysterious story to share.

During the late 1980s/early 1990s (before the digital age of photography as we now know it) a gentleman customer regularly brought in 35 mm film to be developed, processed, and printed. He was a fairly good photographer but, nevertheless, not a professional.

On several occasions, he brought in blurry photos. He had used the same camera and insisted that the camera shop continue to print his photos even though they turned out fuzzy each time.

The owner of Rudd's, Carol Clements, insisted there was something in the fuzzy photos, a figure of some sort, but it just was not clear enough to make out. Shop employees and fellow photographers "discussed each and every print that the customer brought in to us," she said, "and we all kept trying to explain it away as what's known as a *light flare* on the print. We, too, kept explaining to the customer that there was just nothing there! Well, let me rephrase that . . . we could see there was *something* there, but nothing in focus enough to see."

Nonetheless, the customer was adamant that he was taking photos of something he could clearly see with his own eyes. Some of the photos had obviously been taken with a flash; others had not. Either way, it was apparent that all the photos had been taken in the dark, each turning out with nothing of substance to print on the paper.

Carol tirelessly and most often reluctantly continued to print the negatives, as per the loyal customer's request, each and every time he brought them in. "I just felt like he was wasting his money." She paused. "Until one day . . . one day there was something there! It was a figure of some sort that showed up on one of the prints."

The man was overjoyed!

The lab technician at the shop admitted that yes, there was *something* there, but it could not be determined just *what* it was.

The gentleman insisted that he knew exactly not *what* but *who* it was, although he wouldn't share that information with the camera shop employees. He insisted that the camera shop send this particular photo to the film company to prove that he was photographing what he himself could see. Even though she was reluctant, Carol granted his request and sent the print to the photo paper manufacturer in New York.

A few days later, the results were in. It was determined that the small blurry object was an unidentified anomaly—one that was *not* caused by a flash or defect in the print paper.

The gentleman reportedly smiled with tears in his eyes and said, "I knew it! I got her!"

When Carol finally questioned the customer about the photo, he decided to share his secret with her. The ecstatic man explained that he knew no one would believe his story unless he had proof . . . proof that his deceased grandmother was visiting him almost nightly. He shared that when she would come, he would snap photos. He could see her with his own eyes, and he wanted to share this with his family members.

Carol framed a large print of the photo for the gentleman, who has since passed. "But," she said, "He stuck with that story until the day he died!"

No one knows if the photograph still exists, but there is one thing for sure. According to the customer, his grandmother's ghost was captured on film!

CHAPTER SEVEN

THE POLTERGEISTS
OF POLO'S

According to many experts in the paranormal field, polter-geists are most commonly and simply known as mischievous spirits; ghosts that play tricks on people, if you will. And Polo's Restaurant of Uptown Greenwood has had their fair share of experiences with a few invisible tricksters.

Located at 328 Main Street, Polo's is one of the most popular dining destinations in Greenwood County. The atmosphere is most welcoming in this quaint yet upscale restaurant. The friendly staff always greets one with true Southern hospitality, and the restaurant's ambiance is that of true character and charm.

Real estate records show that the building was built in 1896 and consisted of the three stories that are still intact today: the top floor, the main floor (where the restaurant is located on street level); and a basement. As one enters the establishment, the dining area is located to the left of the building, and the bar is to the right. There is also sidewalk dining available in front of the establishment.

Past and present restaurant employees were eager to share their ghostly experiences, although they all asked to remain anonymous. Though they have never felt threatened, they added that they have been "creeped out" by some of the odd occurrences. Each individual insisted that even when there is only one person in the restaurant, that person never feels alone.

Each day, it's routine for the wine glass rack to be restocked with clean wine glasses. Restaurant employees report that on a regular basis, the wine glasses in the rack begin to shake and rattle of their own accord, with no one around close enough to touch the rack or the glasses.

Waitresses have allegedly been tapped on the shoulder, and when they turn around, there is no one there—at least no one who can physically be seen. "It's almost like it's a child playing tricks on us," one waitress said. "The hem on my shirt has also been pulled, as if a child were trying to get my attention."

Customers have reported strange goings-on as well. Keys that suddenly disappear after being placed on the bar and dishes such as glasses and saucers being moved from one area of the bar to another are just a couple of things that have allegedly happened. One customer even watched his full glass of sweet tea move slightly to the left, apparently on its own, several times.

A few years back, a local paranormal investigation team was welcomed by the owner. The team captured an electronic voice phenomenon (EVP) recording of what sounded like a man's voice and several recordings of what sounded like children giggling and running. The basement and the restaurant seemed to be the most active paranormal areas of the establishment.

To date, similar unexplained events continue to happen and are now jokingly referred to as the 'Poltergeists of Polo's'.

CHAPTER EIGHT

THE GHOST OF 312 MAIN

There is an empty building centered almost smack dab in the middle of Uptown Greenwood; 312 Main Street is the exact address. Though surrounded by successful businesses, this three-story, well-built structure cannot seem to stay occupied, at least not by the living.

A coffee shop was the most recent establishment to go out of business, and prior to that, a short-lived BBQ restaurant. The most successful and long-lived business was that of a family-owned jewelry store, which was there for forty years or more.

On many occasions, several people have seen a transparent elderly lady with white hair within the building, most recently by a previous employee of the BBQ restaurant. "I didn't see her every day," she shared, "but I saw her often. I am from out of town and have no idea who she is, but she is a well-dressed older woman with beautiful, grayish-white hair."

One day, this employee went upstairs to the top floor, which at the time served as a storage attic. As she ascended the stairs, she felt as if she weren't alone. "I felt as if someone were watching me and following me up the stairs. I turned around, but of course there was no one there. I had locked all the entrance doors the night before, so I knew no one could be in there unless they had broken in. The manager had given me one of her spare keys and said I could come in early and get a few hours' overtime if I cleaned up the attic, so I took her up on it. I had just come in to organize some boxes, sweep and mop the floor, and move some training supplies downstairs. Renovations were being done to the building at the time, so I thought that by going in early, I would be out of the way of the construction crew."

As the young woman shuffled the scattered boxes into a neat stack in the front corner of the room, she noticed a large frame turned with its front facing the wall. She dusted it off, turned it around, and nearly dropped it. It was a photo of a middle-aged woman. Chills ran through her body as she recognized the face as that of the ghostly woman she had periodically seen. Her hair wasn't completely gray in the portrait, but it was the very same face. *This must have been her at a younger age,* the employee thought to herself.

She slowly walked over to the corner to place the photo in a safe location, on the stack of boxes facing up. As she glanced over to the opposite wall, she saw the morning sun shining through the front windows. Particles of dust could be seen dancing in the sun's rays as they shone through the panes.

She glanced over to the other front corner of the room, and there stood the neatly dressed female—never moving, never acknowledging the employee, never making a sound . . . just standing there with her hands clasped in front of her stomach. Panic suddenly set in, and the employee quickly turned to run down the stairs, tripping over a stray box and falling to the dusty hardwood floor. *Surely the noise of my fall will catch the ghostly woman's attention,* she thought as she scrambled to get back on her feet again. She looked back to see that the stranger was no longer there; she was gone. She had vanished as quickly as she'd appeared.

Finally, the employee made her way back down the stairs, frantically latching the attic door from the outside so whoever was up there could not get out.

Other employees started to trickle in for training. Trying to compose herself, the employee was still startled and still somewhat in shock at what had just happened. She simply didn't know what to make of it, so she felt she should keep the incident to herself.

She went behind the bar and made herself a cup of strong coffee, took a deep breath, and convinced herself to relax. She went to the bathroom to splash some cold water on her face before starting the training session. As she refreshed her face, she began to feel better, convincing herself that it may have just been her imagination. She reached for a paper towel, holding her head down to dry the water from around her eyes. She asserted herself, took another deep breath, and then straightened her belt.

As she glanced up to straighten her ponytail, she looked into the mirror to see not her face, but that of the white-haired lady staring back at her. She had a very stern look on her face and did not seem very happy.

Very soon after, this particular employee changed her place of employment and to this day vows to never go into that building again.

Several other workers insist that during the renovation process, lids would be put on large paint cans at the end of the day, and the next morning the cans would be turned over and paint would be spilled on the floor . . . with no one having been there during the night. Paintbrushes were also moved and even hidden from the workers.

The ghostly woman apparently didn't like the changes that were being made to the building. Her portrait has not been seen since the employee placed it on the stack of boxes, and even though 312 Main Street is currently under construction and empty, it is still believed to be "inhabited."

CHAPTER NINE

SPIRITS, ANYONE?

As one of the newest and most successful businesses in Uptown Greenwood, Flynn's on Maxwell Uptown Wine & Beer is one of the hottest spots to visit. Whether you are a wine or beer expert, Flynn's has the spirit you're looking for!

Located at 120 Maxwell Avenue, this business is adjacent to Main Street. The building is over a century old, as it was built in 1908, and several other establishments have occupied this space before Flynn's. The ghostly goings-on have yet to be explained by the current owners.

Flynn's offers unique and favorite beers and wine, but according to owner Debbie Flynn, those aren't the only *spirits* that seem to be around. On several occasions, Debbie's motion-detecting alarm system alerted the police department that there was motion inside the store; however, video evidence showed no human activity or movement, only "floating orbs" that seemed to trigger the system. In the paranormal world, orbs are defined as small circles of energy that may or may not contain a spirit. Some believe that faces can be seen inside of the circle while others put no trust in orbs and simply dismiss them as particles of dust, which on many occasions may be misidentified as orbs. However, it is agreed by most that tiny dust particles would not set off a motion alarm system.

Another bizarre occurrence that has taken place at Flynn's happened on the top floor, where very few people go. However, Debbie explained that she herself makes regular trips to the top floor, which is currently used as an attic and storage area. "I have been up there several times since the holiday season," she said, "and we have a large Christmas wreath hung up on the wall there, as that is where we store it in the off-season. Well, the last few times I've been up there, the lights on the wreath were off, but on one occasion when I went up there, the lights on the wreath were blinking on and off, and no one had plugged it in. I just can't explain it!"

Still puzzled and confused, Debbie has tried every way she can think of to explain the mysterious incident, but to no avail.

Hundreds of patrons visit this business on a regular basis, yet few may be aware of these odd occurrences that have taken place.

Are there truly invisible entities lurking in this old building? Are the circles seen floating in the air merely dust particles, or could they actually be tiny balls of active energy on a mission from the spirit world? Visitors will have to come to their own conclusions, and one may get a taste of spirits other than just wine or beer when entering Flynn's on Maxwell.

CHAPTER TEN

"ALL ABOARD!"

G reenwood was once a very busy railroad town and helped build America by way of the rails. Five different railroads lay the base for a booming economy and an influx of travelers and settlers to the City of Greenwood during the early 1900s. By 1930, Greenwood had become the center of South Carolina railroad travel, playing host to a greater number of rail lines than any other city in the state. Union Station was located in the middle of the city square and was the central location for parades, political speeches, and rallies, not to mention extensive freight and passenger travel. The very last train rumbled through the city square in 1982.[2]

Located at 908 Main Street South, the Railroad Historical Center is actually in a separate location yet is still part of the Museum in Greenwood. Although it is considered part of Uptown Greenwood, it is about three blocks from the main square, less than a five-minute walk or a minute's drive from the main hub of the uptown area.

---

2   Stacy Thompson and Bethany Wade, *Images of America: Greenwood (Charleston, South Carolina: Arcadia Publishing, 2014), 31.*

Strange things have been said to happen on the train cars that now stand motionless on tracks that lead to nowhere.

Each year, hundreds of elementary school children visit the center as part of educational field trips. On one such occasion, a child asked the tour guide about the man holding the lantern and motioning for him to come to him. No man could be seen by anyone but this one child. The pointed to show his classmates the man, but no one else could see him. He described him to be a regular-size man with a big, thick, curled-up mustache and wearing a gray-striped railroad hat, a gray vest with a white shirt, gray pants, and shiny black shoes. Still, no one could see the man but this one little boy.

As the young tourist began to run toward this mysterious, apparently invisible man, he suddenly shouted and threw his hands up in the air as if to question what had happened. "He's gone! He just disappeared!" yelled the boy to his classmates. He had a very scared and confused look on his face and continued to insist that the man was indeed there. "I saw him! I heard him, and I almost touched him!" cried the puzzled child. The other children were laughing loudly at him now. As the tour guide settled the group of children down, she led them onto the rail car where they continued their tour. However, it seemed that no one would ever be able to convince that one student that what he saw was not real.

Others who have taken the train tour have said that as they walked through the different rail cars, they could hear the clink of dishes and soft whispers of muffled conversation. It was as if there were active conversations and activities aboard.

A lonely lady traveler dressed in period clothing and wearing a small, fancy hat has also reportedly been seen on numerous occasions by several different people. According to one of the spectators, this apparition was wearing a long, brown Victorian traveling dress and a large matching brown hat with orange flowers and beads. She was also wearing crocheted gloves and holding a small purse with a chain handle.

One tourist even kept coming back time after time, taking hundreds upon hundreds of photos in order to try to capture this "ghost" that she insisted she repeatedly saw. According to her, this lady traveler is always sitting alone and motionless, gazing sadly out the window, never moving and never acknowledging any of the tourists as they walk through the train.

In recent years, the rail cars have been renovated and other cars have also been added. During the summer months each year, one can visit, tour, and learn about the history of Greenwood's railroads. One might even possibly catch a glimpse or capture a photo of the spirit of that lonely lady traveler!

Shhh . . . listen closely and you may even hear these words: "All aboard!"

IN CLOSING

Well, as you can see, Uptown Greenwood has its share of ghostly happenings, spirit sightings, and spooky tales.

Whether they are folklore, actual visitors from the spirit world, or just the vivid imaginations of those who choose to believe, the stories can be very intriguing and mysterious.

Please visit these businesses and let them know that you would like to meet the ghosts of Uptown Greenwood—after all, it's obvious that there are more than flowers blooming in Greenwood!

ABOUT THE AUTHOR

Marjorie LaNelle is a native of Ninety Six, South Carolina. She and her husband, Andy, reside in Greenwood County and have three children and three grandchildren. Marjorie earned her degree in business administration from Forrest Junior College.

Marjorie has been writing for as long as she can remember, and her writing as well as her photography have been published in *The Greenwood Magazine*. She is the former editor for www.Gwdtoday.com and has penned over fifteen books and hundreds of poems and songs, but this is her first published book. Her own experiences and interest in unexplained phenomena inspired her to share Greenwood's intriguing stories with others in *Ghost Stories of Uptown Greenwood*.

Made in the USA
Monee, IL
25 September 2020